THIS QUIET TIME JOURNAL BELONGS TO

_____

START DATE

_____

Whatever you do today,
make time with Jesus your one thing alone.

welcome

Can you imagine what your life would be like if you jumped out of bed every morning looking forward to your time with Jesus?

No more snoozing the alarm, no more guilt for missing your Quiet Time, no more shame for not measuring up to other people's standards of what your daily devotions should look like.

Just pure, free joy in meeting with Jesus the way God created YOU to connect with Him?

It's possible! Let's get started.

index

This is the message we have heard from Him and proclaim to you, that God is light, and in him is no darkness at all.

1 JOHN 1:5

GETTING
STARTED

let's get started

Hello there!

You and I haven't met yet, but I know one thing about you: you love Jesus, and you want to spend more time with Him.

Okay, maybe that's two things. See, we're already off to a great start!

Let me tell you a secret: I used to struggle with guilt and shame when it came to my Quiet Time. I'd grown up in a Christian family and I knew I was supposed to read my Bible and pray every day, but sometimes I slept in, or I forgot, or I just didn't want to. And when I failed, I felt like a failure, and I avoided God, which only made everything worse. Eventually, I'd confess my apathy to Him and try again, starting this cycle all over again. I really wanted to spend time with Jesus, but I just couldn't be consistent.

The turning point came when I realized that there is no one-size-fits-all Quiet Time formula prescribed in the Bible. We're not told that morning devotions are better than evening devotions or lunchtime devotions, or even sit-in-the-carpool-line devotions.

The truth is, God is after our hearts, not our checklists. God wants us to spend time with Him every day—throughout the day—not just an hour-long appointment in the morning that we promptly check off our list and forget about soon after.

Maybe the problem is we're trying too hard to cram someone else's idea of a Quiet Time into our overfull lives. Jesus had strong words against the man-made rules that suffocate our souls and pile guilt where God meant there to be delight (see Matthew 23).

Instead, Jesus invites us to do the opposite:

> *"Come to me, all you who are weary and burdened, and I will give you rest. Take my yoke upon you and learn from me, for I am gentle and humble in heart, and you will find rest for your souls."*
> **Matthew 11:28-19**

Rest. Freedom. Joy.

They're all ours when we find our way in Jesus' presence.

let's get started

HOW TO USE THIS JOURNAL

Once we break out of the formulaic Quiet Time box, we can experience the joy of Jesus' presence in many fun, creative, little ways. That's what I finally discovered in my journey with Jesus, and that's what I want for you too.

That's what this journal will help you do.

In the first section, I invite you to learn from your past Quiet Time experiences and create a Quiet Time plan that fits your unique life. You'll find worksheets that walk you through a scientific process of habit formation, and I think you'll be pleasantly surprised to find how simple this is.

The next section is filled with journal sheets that guide you through the daily practice of reading a Bible verse, writing down one thing you learn about God, responding to Him with one thing you'd like to say to Him, and finally committing to one small way of living out what you learned. Every five days, you'll find either a memory verse to meditate on or a reflection sheet to help you chronicle what you've learned throughout your Quiet Time journey.

If you have a Bible reading plan already, great! You can use it with the daily journal sheets. If you don't, you'll find one in the Getting Started section, as well as two additional plans in the Bonus section.

Speaking of bonuses, at the back of this journal I've included some of my favorite resources for you. These are completely optional, but I think you'll enjoy choosing whatever works for you. My goal is to help women enjoy time with Jesus every day, and I'm constantly creating new resources on my website at onethingalone.com. But I've curated some extra goodies that go along with this journal, which you'll find at myonethingalone.com/journal-goodies.

In closing, let me remind us of what God said to the Israelites thousands of years ago, which is just as true for us today:

> *"You will seek me and find me when you seek me with all your heart. I will be found by you,"*
> *declares the Lord.*
> **Jeremiah 29:13-14 NIV**

No more waiting for the perfect time and place. God invites us to come to Him as we are. Whatever that looks like for you in this season of life, seek Him. Make time with Jesus your one thing alone.

With much joy,

Asheritah

One thing I ask from the Lord, this only do I seek: that I may dwell in the house of the Lord all the days of my life, to gaze on the beauty of the Lord and to seek him in his temple

PSALM 27:4

discover *your best Quiet Time method*

Take some time to reflect on why time with Jesus is important to you, what's worked for you in the past, and what potential challenges you'll face in your new Quiet Time habit.

MOTIVATION

Why is Quiet Time with Jesus important to me?

What will my life look like if I spend time with Jesus every day?

METHOD

I can learn from my past Quiet Time experiences:

What I enjoyed:	What I didn't enjoy:	What I want to do differently:
What worked well:	What didn't work:	

This is what my ideal Quiet Time would look like:

CHALLENGES

In my current season, these are the challenges I'm facing:

Time-related challenges:	Place-related challenges:	Other challenges:

plan *your Quiet Time*

Every woman can enjoy consistent Quiet Time with Jesus, and the tiny habit method can help. I've adapted this simple approach to habit formation, inspired by Stanford behavior scientist BJ Fogg, to a daily Quiet Time, but you can also use it for any spiritual habit in your life.

 1 **MAKE YOUR HABIT TINY**

We've all made grandiose goals like "Read the Bible for an hour a day," but failure is quick to follow because we're trying to do too much too soon. Instead, start small. Choose a Quiet Time habit that takes 30 seconds or less. For example, you could start by reading just one verse a day, writing one observation, or writing a one-sentence prayer. This is the approach taken in the daily journal sheets that follow, but if you'd like to create another tiny Quiet Time habit, feel free to use the prompt below.

What is one tiny Quiet Time habit I'd like to try?

2 **LINK IT TO AN ESTABLISHED HABIT**

The hardest part of any new habit is getting started, so create momentum by linking your new tiny habit to an established habit (like brushing your teeth, making coffee, or eating lunch). When possible, store your Bible and journal in the same place to transition more easily.

What are some daily habits that come easily to me?

Where does Quiet Time fit naturally in my life? What habit or routine does it come after?

Create your Quiet Time plan below, linking your tiny habit to an established habit.

After I _____,

I will _____.

plan *your Quiet Time*

 3 **CELEBRATE YOUR WINS**

Don't skip this step! God wired our brains to seek out what feels good, and celebrating reinforces good habits. Whenever you've successfully completed your tiny Quiet Time habit, take a moment to celebrate your victory. It could be as simple as saying, "I did it!", doing a happy dance, or shouting aloud "Hallelujah!" Yes, it might feel silly, but it works! This will reinforce the subconscious message that Quiet Time is pleasurable, which will make you more consistent.

How will I celebrate each day?

Additionally, you may want to set up rewards for yourself when you've hit a long streak, like 5 days in a row, 30 days total, or when you've finished filling out this journal. Yep, sounds simple, but it will give your brain something to look forward to. Our greatest reward will always be Jesus Himself—knowing Him, loving Him, and growing closer to Him. But sometimes tangible goodies help too, especially when they reinforce your Quiet Time habit. Consider a new journal, coloring pens, worship album, study Bible, or a ticket to a women's retreat.

How will I celebrate long streaks?

Some of us are motivated by trackers. If that's you, make sure to check out the floral Quiet Time tracker included in this journal.

tweak *your daily Quiet Time plan*

Count out 10 days from today and circle that date on your calendar. Then come back and answer the questions below.

◆ ◆ ◆ ◆ ◆ ◆ ◆ ◆ ◇

VICTORIES

What's working well with my Quiet Time plan?

CHALLENGES

What challenges am I facing?

What do I need to adjust?

MOVING FORWARD

What's my new Quiet Time plan for this season?

track *your Quiet Time habits*

Sometimes visual trackers help us see just how far we've come. If you're a checklist kind of person, consider tracking your Quiet Time habit by coloring a leaf every day you spend time with Jesus.

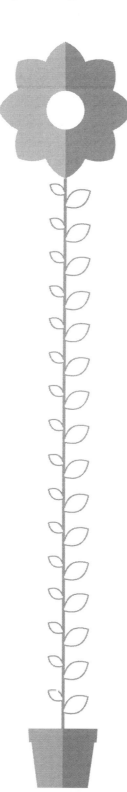
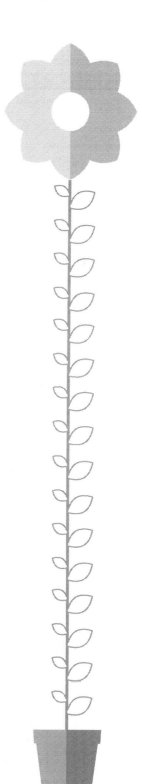

sample journal page

Your journal is your own to fill out as you please. No one will be checking it. But if you're looking for direction a completed page could look like this:

---

today 02 / 18 / 2019

THE SCRIPTURE PASSAGE IS: Matthew 26:6-7, 10

Now when Jesus was at Bethany in the house of Simon the leper, a woman came up to him with an alabaster flask of very expensive ointment, and she poured it on his head as he reclined at table (...) But Jesus, aware of this, said to them, "Why do you trouble the woman? For she has done a beautiful thing to me.

1 What's one thing I learn about God in this passage?

Jesus is not caught up in external appearances; He sees the heart, and when I worship Him from the heart, it's a beautiful and acceptable sacrifice.

2 What's one thing I want to say to God?

Thank You, Jesus, for receiving me into Your presence with open arms. Help me worship You with everything I am and everything I have. I am Yours.

3 What's one thing God is calling me to do?

This week, I want to spend a few quiet moments with Jesus before I go to bed each night, so I'll put my phone away at 8pm and keep my Bible and journal open on my nightstand so I can sit with Him undistracted.

1 John *30-day reading plan*

1	1 John 1:1-4	☐	16	1 John 3:9-10	☐
2	1 John 1:5-7	☐	17	1 John 3:11-15	☐
3	1 John 1:8-10	☐	18	1 John 3:16-18	☐
4	1 John 2:1-2	☐	19	1 John 3:19-24	☐
5	1 John 2:3-6	☐	20	1 John 4:1-3	☐
6	1 John 2:7-8	☐	21	1 John 4:4-6	☐
7	1 John 2:9-11	☐	22	1 John 4:7-12	☐
8	1 John 2:12-14	☐	23	1 John 4:13-17	☐
9	1 John 2:15-17	☐	24	1 John 4:18-21	☐
10	1 John 2:18-20	☐	25	1 John 5:1-5	☐
11	1 John 2:21-23	☐	26	1 John 5:6-9	☐
12	1 John 2:24-27	☐	27	1 John 5:10-12	☐
13	1 John 2:28-29	☐	28	1 John 5:13-15	☐
14	1 John 3:1-3	☐	29	1 John 5:16-17	☐
15	1 John 3:4-8	☐	30	1 John 5:18-21	☐

In Your presence there is fullness of joy; at your right hand are pleasures forevermore.

PSALM 16:11

QUIET TIME
JOURNAL

See what kind of love
the Father has given to us,
that we should be called
children of God; and
so we are.

1 JOHN 3:1

today   /   /

THE SCRIPTURE PASSAGE IS:

1 What's one thing I learn about God in this passage?

2 What's one thing I want to say to God?

3 What's one thing God is calling me to do?

today   /   /

THE SCRIPTURE PASSAGE IS:

1 What's one thing I learn about God in this passage?

2 What's one thing I want to say to God?

3 What's one thing God is calling me to do?

today   /   /

THE SCRIPTURE PASSAGE IS:

1   What's one thing I learn about God in this passage?

2   What's one thing I want to say to God?

3   What's one thing God is calling me to do?

today   /   /

THE SCRIPTURE PASSAGE IS:

1   What's one thing I learn about God in this passage?

2   What's one thing I want to say to God?

3   What's one thing God is calling me to do?

today   /   /

THE SCRIPTURE PASSAGE IS:

1   What's one thing I learn about God in this passage?

2   What's one thing I want to say to God?

3   What's one thing God is calling me to do?

Therefore he is able to
save completely those who
come to God through him,
because he always lives
to intercede for them.

HEBREWS 7:25

today   /   /

THE SCRIPTURE PASSAGE IS:

1 What's one thing I learn about God in this passage?

2 What's one thing I want to say to God?

3 What's one thing God is calling me to do?

today   /   /

THE SCRIPTURE PASSAGE IS:

1 What's one thing I learn about God in this passage?

2 What's one thing I want to say to God?

3 What's one thing God is calling me to do?

today   /   /

THE SCRIPTURE PASSAGE IS:

1 What's one thing I learn about God in this passage?

2 What's one thing I want to say to God?

3 What's one thing God is calling me to do?

today / /

THE SCRIPTURE PASSAGE IS:

1 What's one thing I learn about God in this passage?

2 What's one thing I want to say to God?

3 What's one thing God is calling me to do?

today   /   /

THE SCRIPTURE PASSAGE IS:

1 What's one thing I learn about God in this passage?

2 What's one thing I want to say to God?

3 What's one thing God is calling me to do?

reflection

Use this page to reflect on what you're learning and write out a prayer of worship.

VICTORIES

What have I learned about God?

What have I learned about myself?

What tweaks can I make to my tiny Quiet Time habit?

How can I celebrate my Quiet Time wins so far?

WORSHIP

Offer God a prayer of worship, praise, gratitude, or rededication. Write out your words to Him here.

today / /

THE SCRIPTURE PASSAGE IS:

1 What's one thing I learn about God in this passage?

2 What's one thing I want to say to God?

3 What's one thing God is calling me to do?

today   /   /

THE SCRIPTURE PASSAGE IS:

1 What's one thing I learn about God in this passage?

2 What's one thing I want to say to God?

3 What's one thing God is calling me to do?

today   /   /

THE SCRIPTURE PASSAGE IS:

1 What's one thing I learn about God in this passage?

2 What's one thing I want to say to God?

3 What's one thing God is calling me to do?

today / /

THE SCRIPTURE PASSAGE IS:

1 What's one thing I learn about God in this passage?

2 What's one thing I want to say to God?

3 What's one thing God is calling me to do?

today   /   /

THE SCRIPTURE PASSAGE IS:

1 What's one thing I learn about God in this passage?

2 What's one thing I want to say to God?

3 What's one thing God is calling me to do?

Heaven and earth
will pass away,
but my words will
not pass away.

LUKE 21:33

today   /   /

THE SCRIPTURE PASSAGE IS:

1 What's one thing I learn about God in this passage?

2 What's one thing I want to say to God?

3 What's one thing God is calling me to do?

today   /   /

THE SCRIPTURE PASSAGE IS:

◆ **1** What's one thing I learn about God in this passage?

◆ **2** What's one thing I want to say to God?

◆ **3** What's one thing God is calling me to do?

today   /   /

THE SCRIPTURE PASSAGE IS:

1 What's one thing I learn about God in this passage?

2 What's one thing I want to say to God?

3 What's one thing God is calling me to do?

today   /   /

THE SCRIPTURE PASSAGE IS:

1   What's one thing I learn about God in this passage?

2   What's one thing I want to say to God?

3   What's one thing God is calling me to do?

today　　/　/

THE SCRIPTURE PASSAGE IS:

1 What's one thing I learn about God in this passage?

2 What's one thing I want to say to God?

3 What's one thing God is calling me to do?

reflection

Use this page to reflect on what you're learning and write out a prayer of worship.

VICTORIES

What have I learned about God?

What have I learned about myself?

What tweaks can I make to my tiny Quiet Time habit?

How can I celebrate my Quiet Time wins so far?

WORSHIP

Offer God a prayer of worship, praise, gratitude, or rededication. Write out your words to Him here.

today　　/　　/

THE SCRIPTURE PASSAGE IS:

1 What's one thing I learn about God in this passage?

2 What's one thing I want to say to God?

3 What's one thing God is calling me to do?

today   /   /

THE SCRIPTURE PASSAGE IS:

1   What's one thing I learn about God in this passage?

2   What's one thing I want to say to God?

3   What's one thing God is calling me to do?

today   /   /

THE SCRIPTURE PASSAGE IS:

1   What's one thing I learn about God in this passage?

2   What's one thing I want to say to God?

3   What's one thing God is calling me to do?

today   /   /

THE SCRIPTURE PASSAGE IS:

1 ◆ What's one thing I learn about God in this passage?

2 ◆ What's one thing I want to say to God?

3 ◆ What's one thing God is calling me to do?

today   /   /

THE SCRIPTURE PASSAGE IS:

1 What's one thing I learn about God in this passage?

2 What's one thing I want to say to God?

3 What's one thing God is calling me to do?

For whatever was written in former days was written for our instruction, that through endurance and through the encouragement of the Scriptures we might have hope.

ROMANS 15:4

today   /   /

THE SCRIPTURE PASSAGE IS:

1 What's one thing I learn about God in this passage?

2 What's one thing I want to say to God?

3 What's one thing God is calling me to do?

today   /   /

THE SCRIPTURE PASSAGE IS:

1   What's one thing I learn about God in this passage?

2   What's one thing I want to say to God?

3   What's one thing God is calling me to do?

today　　/　　/

THE SCRIPTURE PASSAGE IS:

1　What's one thing I learn about God in this passage?

2　What's one thing I want to say to God?

3　What's one thing God is calling me to do?

today / /

THE SCRIPTURE PASSAGE IS:

1   What's one thing I learn about God in this passage?

2   What's one thing I want to say to God?

3   What's one thing God is calling me to do?

today   /   /

THE SCRIPTURE PASSAGE IS:

1 What's one thing I learn about God in this passage?

2 What's one thing I want to say to God?

3 What's one thing God is calling me to do?

reflection

Use this page to reflect on what you're learning and write out a prayer of worship.

VICTORIES

What have I learned about God?

What have I learned about myself?

What tweaks can I make to my tiny Quiet Time habit?

How can I celebrate my Quiet Time wins so far?

WORSHIP

Offer God a prayer of worship, praise, gratitude, or rededication. Write out your words to Him here.

today   /   /

THE SCRIPTURE PASSAGE IS:

1 What's one thing I learn about God in this passage?

2 What's one thing I want to say to God?

3 What's one thing God is calling me to do?

today   /   /

THE SCRIPTURE PASSAGE IS:

1   What's one thing I learn about God in this passage?

2   What's one thing I want to say to God?

3   What's one thing God is calling me to do?

today   /   /

THE SCRIPTURE PASSAGE IS:

1   What's one thing I learn about God in this passage?

2   What's one thing I want to say to God?

3   What's one thing God is calling me to do?

today   /   /

THE SCRIPTURE PASSAGE IS:

1 What's one thing I learn about God in this passage?

2 What's one thing I want to say to God?

3 What's one thing God is calling me to do?

today   /   /

THE SCRIPTURE PASSAGE IS:

1 What's one thing I learn about God in this passage?

2 What's one thing I want to say to God?

3 What's one thing God is calling me to do?

The LORD your God is in your midst, a mighty one who will save; he will rejoice over you with gladness; he will quiet you by his love; he will exult over you with loud singing.

ZEPHANIAH 3:17

today   /   /

THE SCRIPTURE PASSAGE IS:

1 What's one thing I learn about God in this passage?

2 What's one thing I want to say to God?

3 What's one thing God is calling me to do?

today   /   /

THE SCRIPTURE PASSAGE IS:

1   What's one thing I learn about God in this passage?

2   What's one thing I want to say to God?

3   What's one thing God is calling me to do?

today   /   /

THE SCRIPTURE PASSAGE IS:

1 What's one thing I learn about God in this passage?

2 What's one thing I want to say to God?

3 What's one thing God is calling me to do?

today   /   /

THE SCRIPTURE PASSAGE IS:

1 What's one thing I learn about God in this passage?

2 What's one thing I want to say to God?

3 What's one thing God is calling me to do?

today   /   /

THE SCRIPTURE PASSAGE IS:

1 What's one thing I learn about God in this passage?

2 What's one thing I want to say to God?

3 What's one thing God is calling me to do?

reflection

Use this page to reflect on what you're learning and write out a prayer of worship.

VICTORIES

What have I learned about God?

What have I learned about myself?

What tweaks can I make to my tiny Quiet Time habit?

How can I celebrate my Quiet Time wins so far?

WORSHIP

Offer God a prayer of worship, praise, gratitude, or rededication. Write out your words to Him here.

today   /   /

THE SCRIPTURE PASSAGE IS:

1 What's one thing I learn about God in this passage?

2 What's one thing I want to say to God?

3 What's one thing God is calling me to do?

today   /   /

THE SCRIPTURE PASSAGE IS:

1   What's one thing I learn about God in this passage?

2   What's one thing I want to say to God?

3   What's one thing God is calling me to do?

today   /   /

THE SCRIPTURE PASSAGE IS:

1   What's one thing I learn about God in this passage?

2   What's one thing I want to say to God?

3   What's one thing God is calling me to do?

today   /   /

THE SCRIPTURE PASSAGE IS:

1 What's one thing I learn about God in this passage?

2 What's one thing I want to say to God?

3 What's one thing God is calling me to do?

today   /   /

THE SCRIPTURE PASSAGE IS:

1   What's one thing I learn about God in this passage?

2   What's one thing I want to say to God?

3   What's one thing God is calling me to do?

Every word of God proves
true; he is a shield to those
who take refuge in him.

PROVERBS 30:5

today / /

THE SCRIPTURE PASSAGE IS:

1 What's one thing I learn about God in this passage?

2 What's one thing I want to say to God?

3 What's one thing God is calling me to do?

today   /   /

THE SCRIPTURE PASSAGE IS:

1   What's one thing I learn about God in this passage?

2   What's one thing I want to say to God?

3   What's one thing God is calling me to do?

today   /   /

THE SCRIPTURE PASSAGE IS:

1   What's one thing I learn about God in this passage?

2   What's one thing I want to say to God?

3   What's one thing God is calling me to do?

today   /   /

THE SCRIPTURE PASSAGE IS:

1 What's one thing I learn about God in this passage?

2 What's one thing I want to say to God?

3 What's one thing God is calling me to do?

today   /   /

THE SCRIPTURE PASSAGE IS:

1   What's one thing I learn about God in this passage?

2   What's one thing I want to say to God?

3   What's one thing God is calling me to do?

reflection

Use this page to reflect on what you're learning and write out a prayer of worship.

VICTORIES

What have I learned about God?

What have I learned about myself?

What tweaks can I make to my tiny Quiet Time habit?

How can I celebrate my Quiet Time wins so far?

WORSHIP

Offer God a prayer of worship, praise, gratitude, or rededication. Write out your words to Him here.

today   /   /

THE SCRIPTURE PASSAGE IS:

1   What's one thing I learn about God in this passage?

2   What's one thing I want to say to God?

3   What's one thing God is calling me to do?

today   /   /

THE SCRIPTURE PASSAGE IS:

◆ **1** What's one thing I learn about God in this passage?

◆ **2** What's one thing I want to say to God?

◆ **3** What's one thing God is calling me to do?

today / /

THE SCRIPTURE PASSAGE IS:

1 What's one thing I learn about God in this passage?

2 What's one thing I want to say to God?

3 What's one thing God is calling me to do?

today   /   /

THE SCRIPTURE PASSAGE IS:

1 What's one thing I learn about God in this passage?

2 What's one thing I want to say to God?

3 What's one thing God is calling me to do?

today / /

THE SCRIPTURE PASSAGE IS:

1 What's one thing I learn about God in this passage?

2 What's one thing I want to say to God?

3 What's one thing God is calling me to do?

Let me hear in the morning of your steadfast love, for in you I trust. Make me know the way I should go, for to you I lift up my soul.

PSALM 143:8

today   /   /

THE SCRIPTURE PASSAGE IS:

1 What's one thing I learn about God in this passage?

2 What's one thing I want to say to God?

3 What's one thing God is calling me to do?

today   /   /

THE SCRIPTURE PASSAGE IS:

1   What's one thing I learn about God in this passage?

2   What's one thing I want to say to God?

3   What's one thing God is calling me to do?

today   /   /

THE SCRIPTURE PASSAGE IS:

1   What's one thing I learn about God in this passage?

2   What's one thing I want to say to God?

3   What's one thing God is calling me to do?

today   /   /

THE SCRIPTURE PASSAGE IS:

1 What's one thing I learn about God in this passage?

2 What's one thing I want to say to God?

3 What's one thing God is calling me to do?

today   /   /

THE SCRIPTURE PASSAGE IS:

1 What's one thing I learn about God in this passage?

2 What's one thing I want to say to God?

3 What's one thing God is calling me to do?

reflection

Use this page to reflect on what you're learning and write out a prayer of worship.

VICTORIES

What have I learned about God?

What have I learned about myself?

What tweaks can I make to my tiny Quiet Time habit?

How can I celebrate my Quiet Time wins so far?

WORSHIP

Offer God a prayer of worship, praise, gratitude, or rededication. Write out your words to Him here.

today   /   /

THE SCRIPTURE PASSAGE IS:

1   What's one thing I learn about God in this passage?

2   What's one thing I want to say to God?

3   What's one thing God is calling me to do?

today   /   /

THE SCRIPTURE PASSAGE IS:

1 What's one thing I learn about God in this passage?

2 What's one thing I want to say to God?

3 What's one thing God is calling me to do?

today   /   /

THE SCRIPTURE PASSAGE IS:

1   What's one thing I learn about God in this passage?

2   What's one thing I want to say to God?

3   What's one thing God is calling me to do?

today   /   /

THE SCRIPTURE PASSAGE IS:

1   What's one thing I learn about God in this passage?

2   What's one thing I want to say to God?

3   What's one thing God is calling me to do?

today   /   /

THE SCRIPTURE PASSAGE IS:

1 What's one thing I learn about God in this passage?

2 What's one thing I want to say to God?

3 What's one thing God is calling me to do?

The grass withers,
the flower fades,
but the word of our
God will stand forever.

ISAIAH 40:8

today / /

THE SCRIPTURE PASSAGE IS:

1 What's one thing I learn about God in this passage?

2 What's one thing I want to say to God?

3 What's one thing God is calling me to do?

today / /

THE SCRIPTURE PASSAGE IS:

1 What's one thing I learn about God in this passage?

2 What's one thing I want to say to God?

3 What's one thing God is calling me to do?

today   /   /

THE SCRIPTURE PASSAGE IS:

1 What's one thing I learn about God in this passage?

2 What's one thing I want to say to God?

3 What's one thing God is calling me to do?

today   /   /

THE SCRIPTURE PASSAGE IS:

1 What's one thing I learn about God in this passage?

2 What's one thing I want to say to God?

3 What's one thing God is calling me to do?

today   /   /

THE SCRIPTURE PASSAGE IS:

1 What's one thing I learn about God in this passage?

2 What's one thing I want to say to God?

3 What's one thing God is calling me to do?

reflection

Use this page to reflect on what you're learning and write out a prayer of worship.

VICTORIES

What have I learned about God?

What have I learned about myself?

What tweaks can I make to my tiny Quiet Time habit?

How can I celebrate my Quiet Time wins so far?

WORSHIP

Offer God a prayer of worship, praise, gratitude, or rededication. Write out your words to Him here.

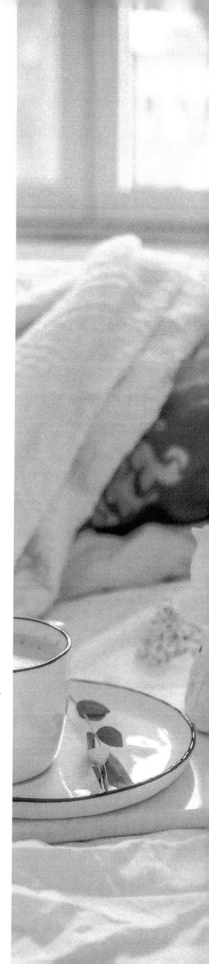

today / /

THE SCRIPTURE PASSAGE IS:

1   What's one thing I learn about God in this passage?

2   What's one thing I want to say to God?

3   What's one thing God is calling me to do?

today   /   /

THE SCRIPTURE PASSAGE IS:

1 What's one thing I learn about God in this passage?

2 What's one thing I want to say to God?

3 What's one thing God is calling me to do?

today   /   /

THE SCRIPTURE PASSAGE IS:

1   What's one thing I learn about God in this passage?

2   What's one thing I want to say to God?

3   What's one thing God is calling me to do?

today   /   /

THE SCRIPTURE PASSAGE IS:

1 What's one thing I learn about God in this passage?

2 What's one thing I want to say to God?

3 What's one thing God is calling me to do?

today   /   /

THE SCRIPTURE PASSAGE IS:

1 What's one thing I learn about God in this passage?

2 What's one thing I want to say to God?

3 What's one thing God is calling me to do?

BONUS
GOODIES

As you've leafed through this journal, you've probably noticed that we've kept the daily journal pages intentionally simple. This is because we're more successful in starting a new habit when we keep things simple, and our habits tiny (as we discussed in the Getting Started section).

But if you've already established a daily Quiet Time, you may be looking for extra ways to deepen your time spent with Jesus. In this case, I've included some of my favorite Quiet Time resources for you here and online at www.myonethingalone.com/journal-goodies.

Here's what's included in this section:

* **Bible reading plans:** In addition to the 30-day reading plan of 1 John included in the Getting Started section, you'll find two extra plans in the pages that follow.

* **Prayer log:** Bring all your requests before the Lord and continue praying for them on a regular basis. As you pray and watch and wait, jot down how God works in each situation. Sometimes He moves in lots of small ways, and we're apt to overlook them if we don't write them down.

* **Gratitude log:** Count your blessings, name them one by one. Remind yourself of God's presence in the big and little things in your life.

* **Memory cards:** Carry God's Word in your heart by cutting out these cards and meditating on these verses while you're washing dishes, running errands, and walking the dog.

Feel free to use whichever resources work for you in this season, and don't feel guilty if you feel like something doesn't fit. Keep it simple. Keep it fun. God wants to transform our time with Him from duty to delight, to change our approach from obligated servant to delighted daughter.

Our relationship with Jesus rests not in our doing but in our being. Being found in Christ. You can stop hustling and rest in the finished work of Jesus on the cross. Simply come to God and say, "I want to delight in You. I want to find joy in Your Word. I want to want You more than anything else in life." Whatever else you long for in life, may time with Jesus become your one thing alone.

"One thing I ask from the Lord, this only do I seek: that I may dwell in the house of the Lord all the days of my life, to gaze on the beauty of the Lord and to seek him in his temple?" (Psalm 27:4 NIV).

rest for weary women *Bible reading plan*

We live in an era of unprecedented busyness. Countless dings and tasks compete for our attention, and it doesn't seem to matter how much we get done in a day, there's always still more to do when our head hits the pillow.

Friends, we're not doomed to a life of constant rushing. Let's learn to experience God's rest in the midst of our busyness, not by escaping our work but by trusting His strength in the midst of it all.

WEEK 1:
Receiving God's Sabbath Rest Today

Genesis 2:2-3	☐
Exodus 20:8-11	☐
Exodus 23:12	☐
Mark 2:23-28	☐
Hebrews 4:1-11	☐

WEEK 2:
Learning to Rest from Striving

Isaiah 43:1-7	☐
John 1:10-16	☐
Matthew 11:28-30	☐
Luke 18:9-14	☐
Mark 6:30-32	☐

WEEK 3:
Trusting God as Means of Rest

Isaiah 40:25-31	☐
Psalm 118:1-17	☐
Psalm 46:10	☐
Isaiah 30:15-18	☐
Psalm 20:1-9	☐

WEEK 4:
Working from a Place of Rest

Psalm 127	☐
2 Corinthians 2:14-16	☐
Ephesians 2:6-10	☐
Colossians 1:28-29	☐
Philippians 1:3-6	☐

real faith meets real life *Bible reading plan*

The book of James was written to first-century Christians from the early Jerusalem church who were scattered throughout the known world after Stephen's death. As their former pastor, James provides practical instruction that's as applicable today as it was 2,000 years ago.

Who should you sit with at a party? What should you say about that back-biting friend? How should you react when you get passed over for that promotion?

Issues unique to our 21st century? Not at all. Let's dig into James.

WEEK 1:
Trials, Temptations, and Faith in Action

James 1:1-12	☐
James 1:13-18	☐
James 1:19-27	☐
James 2:1-13	☐
James 2:14-26	☐

WEEK 2:
Wisdom and Worldliness

James 3:1-12	☐
James 3:13-18	☐
James 4:1-3	☐
James 4:4-10	☐
James 4:11-12	☐

WEEK 3:
Boasting, Prayer, and Faithfulness

James 4:13-17	☐
James 5:1-6	☐
James 5:7-12	☐
James 5:13-18	☐
James 5:19-20	☐

prayer log

Date	Prayer	God at Work

prayer log

Date	Prayer	God at Work

prayer log

Date	Prayer	God at Work

prayer log

Date	Prayer	God at Work

gratitude log

1

2

3

4

5

6

7

8

9

10

11

12

13

14

15

16

17

18

19

20

21

22

23

24

25

26

27

28

29

30

31

gratitude log

1
2
3
4
5
6
7
8
9
10
11
12
13
14
15
16
17
18
19
20
21
22
23
24
25
26
27
28
29
30
31

gratitude log

1
2
3
4
5
6
7
8
9
10
11
12
13
14
15
16
17
18
19
20
21
22
23
24
25
26
27
28
29
30
31

gratitude log

1

2

3

4

5

6

7

8

9

10

11

12

13

14

15

16

17

18

19

20

21

22

23

24

25

26

27

28

29

30

31

And walk in love, as
Christ loved us and
gave himself up for
us, a fragrant offering
and sacrifice to God.

EPHESIANS 5:2

As the Father has loved
me, so have I loved you.
Abide in my love.

JOHN 15:9 ESV

But God demonstrates
his own love for us in this:
While we were still sinners,
Christ died for us.

ROMANS 5:8 NIV

And so we know and
rely on the love God
has for us. God is love.
Whoever lives in love lives
in God, and God in them.

1 JOHN 4:16 NIV

But you, O Lord, are
a God merciful and
gracious, slow to anger
and abounding in steadfast
love and faithfulness.

PSALM 86:15 ESV

For the word of God is alive
and active. Sharper than
any double-edged sword, it
penetrates even to dividing
soul and spirit, joints and
marrow; it judges the thoughts
and attitudes of the heart.

HEBREWS 4:12 NIV

Heaven and earth will
pass away, but my words
will not pass away.

MATTHEW 24:35 ESV

WHAT'S
NEXT

WHAT'S NEXT

You're finished! Yay!! You may be wondering, "Now what? Where do I go from here?"

Here are a few ideas:

1. Reflect on what you've learned about God, yourself, and your Quiet Time. Then use the Quiet Time Tweaks worksheet to adapt for this next season of your life. Remember to keep your plan simple and incorporate lots of fun ideas to keep it fresh. Find 120+ creative devo ideas at www.myOneThingAlone.com/journal-goodies

2. Keep reading God's Word
You can use a simple notebook and write out the "one thing" framework you've learned or order another Quiet Time Journal for this next season.

3. Share with a friend. Feel free to use the stationary pages on the following pages to share with a friend what you've learned over the last few months and encourage her as she seeks to cultivate consistent time with Jesus too.

4. Drop us a note. Tell us how this journal has helped you in your personal Quiet Time, and mail it to us. We love getting fun mail, and we might just send you something back if you do.

Whatever your next steps look like, I hope you continue to seek Jesus and make time with Him your one thing alone.

With much joy,

Asheritah

encourage a friend

A NOTE OF ENCOURAGEMENT

Use this page to write a note of encouragement to a friend. Look back over your journaling pages from the last few months and share something you've learned – perhaps a Scripture application that touched your heart or a verse you've carried with you. Offer something that may encourage her in her own Quiet Time habit.

interact *with us*

KEEP IN TOUCH!

We want to hear from you! Use this page to share how this journal helped you in your personal Quiet Time. Cut out the bottom portion, jot down a few quick thoughts, and mail it to us. We love getting fun mail, and if you make our day with a special note, we just might send you something back!

One Thing Alone Ministries | 1370 Main St, PO Box 330 | Lakemore, OH 44250

notes

notes

notes

notes

notes

notes

notes

notes

notes

notes

notes

notes

notes

notes

notes

Made in the USA
Lexington, KY
21 September 2019